The Relationship Job
WORKBOOK

This Workbook is a 90-Day Guide for individuals who want to be in a happy, healthy, committed, and long-term relationship that they deserve.

A RELATIONSHIP IS A JOB
AND A JOB AIN'T NOTHING BUT WORK!™

KNOWLEDGE POWER BOOKS

Copyright by Terry Campbell 2019

All rights reserved. In accordance with the U.S. Copyright Act of 1976, the scanning, uploading, and electronic sharing of any part of this book without the permission of the publisher is unlawful piracy and theft of the author's intellectual property. If you would like to use material from this book (other than for review purpose), prior written permission must be obtained by contacting the publisher at books@knowledgepowerinc.com.

Thank you for your support of the author's rights.

ISBN: 978-1-950936-13-7 (Paperback)
ISBN: 978-1-950936-14-4 (Ebook)
Library of Congress Control Number: 2019908844

Edited by: Steve Robinson
Cover Design: Angie Ayala
Photography: Juan Roberts, Creative Lunacy, Inc.
Literary Director: Sandra L. Slayton

Published by:

KP Publishing Company
A Division of Knowledge Power Communications, Inc.
Valencia, CA 91355
www.knowledgepowerinc.com

Printed in the United States of America

"Love is patient, love is kind. It does not envy, it does not boast, it is not proud. It does not dishonor others, it is not self-seeking, it is not easily angered, and it keeps no record of wrongs. Love does not delight in evil but rejoices with the truth. It always protects, always trusts, always hopes, and always perseveres. Love never fails."

—1Corinthians 13:4-8

DEDICATION

I dedicate this book to my beautiful wife, Tamara.

April 14, 2018, is proof that *The Relationship Job* works. It was the day I married my love, my lover, my friend, and best friend—the one I attracted.

Tamara, I've loved you since the day I met you. God gave you to me as His gift and He knew exactly what He was doing when He sent you to me. God knew that it would take a strong and special woman to help guide me. When God sent you to me, I was emotionally broken and mentally damaged by love. Then you came along and looked passed my emptiness, my brokenness, my shallow heart, and you loved me anyway. Your love filled me up with everything I was missing. Every day and in every way you make me want to be a better man. You are truly my shining star, my guiding light, and my love fantasy that, has become a reality. The love I have for you keeps growing and growing every day.

I love you, Tamara. To say, "I DO" is the same as saying "I WILL," and I will love you passionately every day. I will honor you every chance I get, I will respect you every minute of every hour, and I will fight for your love always. I will also love and care for Jayahni, Jacobi, Joziah, Jacob, and Jynasis. Thank you for being what I need at all times.

"Remember that work is the most appropriate context for us to evolve and grow as human beings, because through work it is possible to develop skills, contribute to the progress of others, improve relationships and know your own limitations."

—Carlos Eduardo Medeiros de Carvalho

CONTENTS

Dedication — vii
Introduction — xiii

The Reason Why — 1
A Job — 15
A Relationship — 19
Your Potential Partner — 23
You Are the Product, the Business, and the Job — 25
Accepting Differences — 29
A Safe Environment — 31
Unwelcomed Behavior — 33
Interacting With Others — 35
Safe and Sober — 37
Personal Calls, Pagers, Cell Phones — 39
Be on Time — 41
If We Have Plans — 43
Keeping Your Potential Partner Informed — 45
Confidentiality — 47
Going Through Your Things — 49
Work on Your Mind and Body — 51
Extracurricular Activities — 53
Relationships Are "At Will" — 55
Don't Want vs. Want? — 59

Be Specific about What You Want	63
Best Relationship Practices	67
Personal Appearance	71
Intentional Communication	75
Jealousy	81
Keep Aggressive Behavior Away	83
Unacceptable Behavior, Conduct, or Attitude	87
Progressive Communication Take Action System	91

RELATIONSHIP JOB EXERCISES

Don't Want vs. Want?	99
Be Specific about What You Want	101
Best Relationship Practices	105
Personal Appearance	107
Jealousy	111
Keep Aggressive Behavior Away	113
Be the Change You Want to See	115
Evaluations	117
2-Week Evaluation	120
30-Day Evaluation	122
60-Day Evaluation	124
90-Day Evaluation	126
Progressive Communication Take Action Form	129
Acknowledgments	*131*
References	*133*

INTRODUCTION

I've worked in the service and hospitality industry for more than 30+ years, and I've been in some good and some difficult relationships for the past 20+ years as well. Over the years, I've seen people come into my life for either personal reasons or professional reasons. I witnessed people grow in the business, get promoted, and become successful. I've also seen people become complacent, get demoted, get fired, and failed professionally and personally.

I am fortunate to have learned something new from each one that I've come in contact with. Every company that I have worked at gave me a handbook on the first day of the job. These handbooks were designed to provide me with a basic understanding of the job's expectations of what was required of me.

I started to think, what if I use these same techniques that some of the most successful establishments used to train, coach, and develop new potential employees. I thought I could take the outline from the handbooks and apply it to my current relationships. I started to use the same techniques and guess what happened? It worked! I took what I read and combined what I researched over the years to create what I believe is a new, different, and exciting way to communicate with your "potential partner." I took everything that worked in my relationships, in my friends' relationships, combined them and *The Relationship Job* was created. This book is for anyone who wants a happy, healthy, committed long-term relationship.

A Job vs. A Relationship and the correlation between the two was what I designed. I discovered how fascinating it was that these two seemingly different areas of life operated the exact same way.

As an employer, I've hired many employees. I've looked through countless resumes and applications looking for the "best possible candidate." The goal is to find "that right one," who will be a good fit for the job. But; dating is different. (So I assumed.) Dating or a relationship can operate the same way a job does, but differently.

For example, a company usually will send you through one to three interviews before you receive an offer to be hired or not. We're taught that in a relationship, you usually go on one to three dates before the decision is made to officially "give you the offer to start the dating process."

Once employed at this new job, you are immediately placed on a 90-day probationary period. During the 90 days, the most crucial part is the first two weeks. You are usually coupled with a trainer for approximately one or two weeks in your specific position. Usually, you would receive an evaluation at the end of each week. These evaluations are essential, especially if the new hire shows promise of being a good fit. If they demonstrate they're not a good fit for the position, separation should happen before or at the end of the second evaluation. When the new hire survives the first 90 days, then and only then; will you receive all of "the benefits" that are available to you. I was thinking out loud and said to myself *I can use this same format that the Jobs use to help others build and keep their relationships.*

In an effort to find and keep love, I believe we've grown far too polite in our approach. We talk around, over, and under the issue with our potential partner. We're afraid of stepping on toes and scaring each other away, we fail to ask the right questions, set boundaries we need, and have the conversations that are crucial to discerning whether this love is the one we want and deserve.

It's time to flip the script on dancing around the issue! Let's discover how to approach love using our brain while following our hearts.

**—The Real Deal On Love and Men
Michelle McKinney Hammond**

THE REASON WHY

I wrote this book because it saddens me that the teachings of all the men that came before me seemed to have all the answers, but now it has become a lost form of expression. I believe that most of the teachings that these men passed down from generation to generation is now beginning to fade away. There are subtle, basic, and unwritten rules that we were taught to follow as young men and if we are not careful this fantastic art will be forgotten.

The "bros code" is a disrespectful and immature saying that a lot of men adopted as the truth which means "bros before hoes." The real "bros code" I can sum it up in one simple word, Chivalry. Lately it seems that the men who know the truth about chivalry keep it to themselves, but I was wrong. It appears that these men in the past have taught this almost lost technique to a small percentage of other men. I was blessed to have been taught this beautiful technique late in my life and I believe all young men need to know this sooner than later in their life. So I spent years collecting bits of information and converted it to what I believe is desperately needed now.

First men need to understand how to conduct themselves in front of other men. Earl Nightingale teaches us "that you don't get out of life what you want, you get out of life what you are" translation "Like Attracts Like." Example: Winners attract other winners, losers attract other losers, and chivalrous men will attract other chivalrous men.

Women, remember men will only do what you allow them to do to you. I really believe that women don't believe that it's their job to teach men how to respect them outside of sex and/or the bedroom.

Men, please understand that the woman is the prize. He who chooses a women chooses a good thing! She was chosen just for you to be a helper, your helpmate. She is your equal, not your competition, a woman should always be viewed as the queen of the earth, and the only true giver of life.

When I was 19 I decided to move from Louisville, Kentucky to Los Angeles, a place where it never snows and according to the singing group, Tony! Toni! Tone! It never rains. My friend, Shoestring and I bought a one-way ticket on a Greyhound bus to sunny Southern California. On April 29, 1991, I stepped off the bus onto the streets of the sunshine state. I had $1000 dollars in my pocket and a dream. However, in L.A. $1,000 wasn't much.

Shoestring and I quickly ran out of money and was homeless. We slept in a different place almost every night for a few weeks. When I thought I was at my breaking point a divine intervention happened. I was introduced to a man who told me about The Covenant House California.

He said, "Dial the Nine-Line."

"What's the Nine-Line?" I asked.

"The Nine-Line is a toll-free number to a shelter for homeless kids under the age of 21, and I believe they can help you."

I dialed the number. It was to Covenant House. They came and picked up me and my friend, Shoestring, fed us, and gave us a place to sleep.

Covenant House's rules were simple; get a job within 30 days, and you can stay, attend, and participate in all daily meetings (mainly about self-esteem and character-building). But; if you're wasting time, joking around, and not taking the structure seriously, then Covenant House was not the place for you. I quickly got a job, followed all the rules, and met some pretty cool people along the way.

With the help of Covenant House, I was able to gain more confidence in myself, take responsibility for my actions, and stay in L.A. I saved enough money to rent my first apartment. Being on my own made me feel more like a man than I ever felt before. Shortly after settling into my new place, I started to dress nicer, wore better cologne, and my appetite for women was stronger.

Over the years, I was with a few women, but only three of these women I considered my "girlfriends." They all were older than me, so I was like a sponge absorbing everything, and I learned so much from them. These women opened my eyes to a whole new world that I never knew existed.

The first woman taught me how to respect not only her but other women as well. She taught me almost all the things I still use today, also the difference between having sex and making love.

The second woman introduced me to fine wine and dining, and Smooth Jazz. She taught me how to drive, to always open a woman's' door, where I'm supposed to walk when the two of us walked down the street. She also gave me a lot of compliments and that helped me a little more with confidence.

The third girl taught me how to listen to people when they talk and how to talk to people so they'll listen to me. I learned the importance of constant communication, being on time, and "*say what you mean and mean what you say.*"

It seemed that whenever something good was happening in my life, and everything seemed to be going great, the temptation for sex showed up, and I would end up in bed with another woman. I felt unworthy of love so I would do stupid things to sabotage the relationship. I believed growing up without my father, I was never taught how to respect myself, my commitments, or my relationships were some of the reasons for my behavior.

I never was caught cheating, but after a while, I started feeling bad about what I was doing. Even though that wasn't the last time that I cheated, I didn't learn my lesson until my introduction to karma. You might say, I was one of those young men that needed to learn things the hard way.

I was evicted from my apartment and had to move in with my girlfriend at the time. After about a month of living together, it seemed that we argued almost every day. We weren't having sex, and most of our arguments were about her suspicions of my infidelity.

One day, unexpectedly, she told me that we needed to talk (I know now it was a confession), and that she had been sad for a while. "I have been seeing another guy for a couple of months and the last time we were together we had sex."

I stopped breathing, my heart felt like it was going to burst outside of my chest, I was confused and hurt, I forgot about all the crap I had done, and I started to cry. It was the first time I had cried in my adult life. "Ole what a tangled web we weave when we make an attempt to deceive."

I have cheated on women dozens of times in my past relationships but, no one or nothing could've prepared me for the feeling of a broken heart. It finally hit me that I was in love (it was a sick and twisted kind of love, but I was finally in love).

In my past, I had to deal with the heartache of being cheated on, the confusion of being dumped, and the stupidity I felt by being lied to, really opened up my eyes to an indescribable and unexplainable kind of pain. I guess the third time is the charm because I asked myself, *how did I get here again? How did I mess up another relationship?*

I believed that I learned my lesson, and I never wanted to go through that kind of pain again, and most importantly I didn't want to be responsible for causing someone else this kind of pain. I remembered how my mother and my aunts used to say, "you get what you give," which means if you give love, then you'll get love but, the other side of that is if you give crap, then you'll get crap. I now understand the meaning of that word karma.

"Albert Einstein defined insanity as doing the same thing the same way over and over again but expecting a different result."

After six years, I decided to leave sunny California. My goal was to get focused on getting a good job and improve the direction of my life. My first real job was at an upscale restaurant as a cook in Las Vegas, Nevada. On the very first day of the job, during orientation, my manager gave me the employee handbook. He knew I didn't have much experience so he advised me to read it. He also said this book will help me get more familiar with the company, it's core values, their policies and procedures. (I read it from cover to cover). Reading that book was one of the best decisions that I've made.

The employee handbook explained the "do's and dont's" of the company's business. It gave examples of how to fix bad habits, the importance of communication, how your appearance and attitude are a direct reflection of their business. I appreciated the handbook, and it felt like I was learning to speak a new language. It came in handy whenever I had an issue with my managers or my co-workers.

I worked my way up from a cook to a Chef. I worked my butt off for two years before the company offered me the position of a Corporate Traveling Chef. My job was to help open, monitor, and maintain their restaurants' standards. For three years, I developed and coached staff members in multiple locations in California, Arizona, Nevada, Washington, Georgia, and Tennessee.

The traveling job ended when I was in Memphis, Tennessee. I didn't know what to do, so went back home to Kentucky. I decided on my first day back that I wanted to continue my education, so I enrolled in a Culinary Arts program. Shortly after starting, I got a job at The Browns, one of Louisville's Four-Star Hotels. I worked for a very high-end restaurant, The English Grill, located inside of the hotel. On my first day, I received another handbook (yes, I did read it!).

Two years after I graduated with my associates degree, I made the decision to move once again back to Los Angeles. I had grown personally, as well as professionally. As soon as I got back to Los Angeles, I quickly got a job with Jimmy Kimmel Live. I worked Monday to Friday and on weekends I would work as a Private Chef.

I took several pictures with celebrities like Carson Daly, Dave Chappelle, Jimmy Kimmel, Method Man, Marlon Wayans, Marilyn Manson, and others. I was working a dream job and I should've been happy but I wasn't. It did not fulfill me. I felt like something was missing, but I couldn't figure out what.

Ironically the television show that I worked at started to slow down. My work schedule went from 5 days to 3 days a week. At that point, I believe that God was telling me this was a perfect time to make my exit so, I chose to quit the show. I had to swallow my pride and leave Hollywood behind. It wasn't easy, but after about six months, I rediscovered my happiness.

Afterward, I started seeing why I was chosen to work for four- and five-star hotels, bistro-style restaurants, upscale, and casual plus dining restaurants. The one thing that all these different companies had in common was: wait for it, Yup; they all gave me their version of an employee handbook. I received the infamous "handbook" on the first day of work, and each company was serious about setting and maintaining its standards from the beginning.

All the handbooks I read were designed to help me understand more about each business, their beliefs, non-negotiables, expectations, and benefits of the company. They enabled me to ask the right questions of my managers, coworkers, vendors, friends, and customers.

The handbooks also helped me become crystal-clear on the type of employee the companies wanted to keep on board. These books inspired me

THE RELATIONSHIP JOB

Chef Terry and Jimmy Kimmel

Chef Terry, Method Man and Dave Chappelle

Chef Terry and Carson Daly

Chef Terry and Marilyn Manson

Chef Terry and Marlon Wayans

to see the kind of person that I needed to become, and the kind of person that I wanted to work with. I started to notice that I was using what I learned from this handbook to make smarter decisions not only in my professional life but in my personal life as well. Those books guided me to set standards for myself, my family, and my friends. I even noticed that I started making better decisions when dating.

My friends would always tell me that I gave good advice, but I never thought much about it because in my mind, I was just helping a friend out. I didn't do anything with the skill that everyone said I had because I guess I didn't believe in myself enough or I didn't think I could do it.

They would sometimes ask me for advice about dates or dating (I used to call myself The First Date Chef). I think they liked my simple approach to their questions and how I would always give simple and sometimes funny answers that would work.

One day a good friend said to me, "the next time someone asks you for advice, you should record your answer(s) or at least write it down."

"Why?" I asked.

"Because you give good advice, you take what seems to be a complicated question and give it a simple answer," she answered.

"Really!" I said

"Yes, and I believe that you have a gift." She said.

I was always writing down ideas and scenarios for dates, and it still took me several months before I could even believe in myself enough to think I could actually do what my friend was saying.

Two of my friends called to inform me that they started dating again, convinced that they had found "the one." During separate conversations, they both asked me for my advice. Basically; they both said they didn't want to mess things up this time. I remembered what my friend told me a while ago, so I wrote down some basic thought-provoking questions that I usually ask on a date. I always believed that your first three dates should be viewed as three-first dates.

Instead of asking the typical questions like, what do you like to do for fun? What does your perfect day look like? I preferred to focus on subjects that match my strengths and are the opposite of my weaknesses. These questions should help you see how the other person answers questions. It'll help you see the things they want and need to improve on, and most importantly you'll understand how they see themselves. Remember to be fair when asking questions because, there are no perfect people and, if you are looking for something to be wrong, then you'll find it.

HELPFUL QUESTIONS:

Below are important tips on asking the right questions.

1. What are your long term and short-term goals?
2. Are you happy with your job, your work?
3. Where do you see yourself in the next five years?
4. Name two or three techniques that you use to help keep you focused on your goals.
5. What is your six-month plan to help develop yourself?
6. What goals are you most proud of? What goals are you least proud of? Why?
7. What do you most enjoy about your life?
8. What concerns do you have (if any) when it comes receiving negative feedback?
9. What do you see as your top two non-negotiables for dating? Why?
10. What kind of work comes easiest to you?

A relationship is a negotiation, and the two of you have a right to know specific things and more. Your time is valuable and, you don't want to waste their time and most importantly, not to have them waste your time. If the relationship doesn't work it's best to find that out sooner than later. So, ask lots of questions even if you are scared, or if you have to write them down, so you don't forget. Before the end of the date make sure you ask all your questions.

Below are my questions you may use or you may want to create your own. When writing down your questions be honest with yourself.

1. **Do you want the person that you are dating to get to know you, I mean the real you, the good and the "bad side" of you?**

    If so, it allows the other person to decide if they want to continue to be with you or not.

2. **Do you know what you want in a relationship? You must be crystal-clear about what you want!**

    If you meet an ambitious and highly motivated person, and you are unsure about what you want, in my experience, the relationship probably won't work out.

3. **Do you think or believe that you've changed or grown since your previous relationship(s)?**

    You don't want to take the old version of you into this new relationship. It'll never work.

4. **Are you comfortable in uncomfortable situations or questions?**

   Because as soon as you show your standard to another person, you can't ever lower it, and everything you do will be measured by the standard that you set for yourself and your relationship.

5. **Are you prepared to ask a lot of direct questions?**

   If she or he has the potential to be "the one," then you have a right to know what their goals, dreams, and the directions that their life is going, and what they can expect from you in return.

Try to sound natural with your series of questions, let it flow, and try not to sound so rehearsed.

My friends used my advice and it seemed to have worked. One friend discovered that a serious and healthy relationship requires a lot of talking, communicating, and being vulnerable. My other friend, determined that by asking questions, setting standards, and holding the other person accountable to their word; the wrong person will run away and the right person, the one you are supposed to be with, will reveal themselves to you almost every time.

I always explain my format and my simple approach to communication. You have to first know what your standards are and hold yourself to the same high standard that you expect your potential partner to uphold. And never waver (even if it means letting someone go). Always remember, that a relationship is a negotiation, you and your potential partner have to recommit to your relationship Everyday! Everyday! Everyday! No exceptions.

In this handbook, I believe you will find the answers to why relationships work and why they sometimes fall apart. I promise if you follow the instructions and do the work, *The Relationship Job* will get you ready for a serious love affair with your partner, that'll last and it will prepare you for the next level in your relationship. It will help develop your thinking, improve your communication skills, and help you to find the right partner sooner than later. I used the techniques in this book to help me find my wife.

One of the most interesting things that I've learned in my research is that there is a fine line between a job and the basic functions of that job, compared to a relationship and the basic functions of that relationship.

"The best way to discover your greatness is by upgrading your relationships and having goals that are beyond your comfort zone."

—Les Brown

A JOB

Operating at the highest level at your job is not easy, but it's doable. There are many reasons why a company would terminate an employee. But unfortunately, for most newly hired employees, the company doesn't need a reason to let you go. On a job, you are considered "an at-will employee." The description of "at-will" is that you can be terminated at any time without any reason and notice as long as it's within the 90-day probationary period (this is extreme and unlikely to happen, but it's possible).

THAT'S WHY IT'S IMPORTANT TO SET THE STANDARD EARLY ON IN THE EMPLOYMENT.

With that said; most employers need you for a specific reason. In my experience, the company you work for will not terminate you without a serious cause. Most terminations should have a purpose, which means the employee is let go for that specific reason or multiple reasons. Take a look at some of the most common reasons that employees can get terminated from their jobs within the 90-day probationary period.

- Irreconcilable differences
- Incompatibility
- Abandonment
- Alcohol abuse
- Mistreatment to others
- Extreme cruelty
- Emotional abuse
- No call no show
- Neglecting your responsibility
- Fraud
- Money matters
- Lack of communication
- Physical abuse
- Constant arguing
- Unrealistic expectations
- Lack of equality
- Drug Abuse
- Property Damage

"When you prepare yourself everything that's really worthwhile in life comes to us."

—**Earl Nightingale**

A RELATIONSHIP

Operating at a high level in a relationship is not easy but it is doable. Even couples with the best intentions are sometimes unable to overcome their challenges and end up separating.

<u>THAT'S WHY IT'S IMPORTANT TO ADDRESS ISSUES IN YOUR RELATIONSHIP EARLY ON.</u>

Don't wait until issues are beyond fixing before you do something about it. Practice PDA (Public Display of Affection), make intimacy a priority, go on vacations, getaway for the weekend, seek relationship or marriage counseling (even when things seem to be fine) to help preserve your relationship. Try your very best before you decide that things are beyond your control and quit the relationship. When you do this, you can have peace of mind knowing that you tried all of the alternatives before the big step. It doesn't matter whose fault it is for separation in a relationship, and there are no easy ways to do it. Usually, specific grounds are on board before separation is official, and it's unlikely going to be a mutual one.

- Irreconcilable differences
- Incompatibility
- Abandonment
- Alcohol abuse
- Mistreatment to others
- Extreme cruelty
- Emotional abuse
- No call no show
- Neglecting your responsibility
- Fraud
- Money matters
- Lack of communication
- Constant arguing
- Unrealistic expectations
- Lack of equality
- Drug Abuse
- Physical abuse
- Property Damage

"If you want to be a leader who attracts quality people, the key is to become a person of quality yourself."

—Jim Rohn

YOUR POTENTIAL PARTNER

When you're considering someone to be in a relationship with, your potential partner (aka the candidate), the one you've chosen is expected to be around for a long time. However; you must protect yourself from people that will waste your time, play games, or ultimately not be interested in going in the same direction that you are going. To avoid taking the long route and finding out later on that the two of you are not a good fit together, I suggest taking your next relationship seriously by putting your candidate on a 90-day probationary period, so you can evaluate and monitor how well you will fit with one another. Please explain to your potential partner why you're waiting.

HELPFUL TIPS:
<u>You have to be crystal-clear when you let this person know what your expectations, values, and non-negotiables are.</u>

The success in the probationary period will determine if the your potential partner will receive a "permanent position" with you or not.

Your potential partner has 90 days to prove that he or she really wants to do "THE JOB" of making your relationship work. Remember: the first two weeks are the most important. This time will let you know quickly if your potential partner is a right fit for you and <u>yes, there will be a two-week evaluation.</u> The first 30–60–90-day evaluations are equally important for you to evaluate and address all the successes, issues, comments, or concerns involving your new relationship.

BTW:

<u>There will be a 30–60–90-day evaluation.</u>

It doesn't matter how comfortable or close the two of you get with one another, **REMEMBER** your potential partner is still on probation. The 90-day probationary period is based on "performance and results," Period! The evaluation is an opportunity for you to see if your potential partner is going to do what he or she says they are going to do. Here are two examples: Do they show up on time? Do they produce at a high level to the best of their ability? <u>Make sure to watch how they treat you, and most importantly how well they treat themselves.</u> *Never forget that you are the product, the business, and the job.*

The Relationship Job Handbook will provide you with information regarding the beliefs, benefits, practices, procedures, and expectations of a relationship as if it were a product. You should be excited about the contributions you are going to make inside your new relationship and the positive effect that you'll have on everyone around you. My hope for you is that you will find this handbook to be very rewarding, helpful, and needed.

YOU ARE THE PRODUCT, THE BUSINESS, AND THE JOB

This handbook will provide you with some basic, insightful knowledge, and the know-how of a relationship as it operates like an actual Job. You are the Product. You are the Business. You are the Job. Remember you are your own top salesperson. You have to sell your product (aka yourself) Everyday! Everyday! Everyday!

This technique is designed for you to be the best in your relationship. The approach is simply to ensure that you are always improving and learning. You will be able to apply what you have learned over and over again especially where it's needed, in your relationship!

The Relationship Job can also help you if:

- You are dating and believe your relationship isn't going anywhere
- You are in a committed relationship and you want to get married

- you are married and you want a closer relationship with your husband or wife
- or you just want to learn some fun, exciting, useful techniques in your already established relationship

The Relationship Job offers a high level of development, coupled with some proven hospitality standards through verbal and written communication. If you follow the suggestions in this handbook correctly, it can help you as it has many others.

It is designed to provide you the confidence you'll need and will help you after choosing your potential partner. Hopefully, your potential partner is looking to be in a relationship, and not just any relationship but the right relationship, with you! If you are willing to do the work, the reward is a long-lasting, genuine, and productive relationship. Remember to view your relationship as if it is a job for the next 90 days and always remember:

***A RELATIONSHIP IS A JOB AND A JOB AIN'T NOTHING BUT WORK!*™**

"The best person to talk to about the problems in your relationship is the person you're in the relationship with."

—Tony Robbins

ACCEPTING DIFFERENCES

You should be committed to providing an equal opportunity to anyone that appears to be a qualified candidate for you to date. By using the T.E.A.M philosophy (Together Everyone Achieves More) you are committed to achieving excellence through diversity regardless of race, color, age, national origin, ancestry, or creed.

By the time you finish this handbook the new skills, knowledge, and understanding you possess will open new possibilities that you and your potential partner can experience. Accepting cultural differences teaches honor, respect, and values that will overflow onto whomever you come in contact with.

A SAFE ENVIRONMENT

Safety is essential; you will make every effort to provide a safe, comfortable, healthy, and romantic environment for yourself and your potential partner. To assist with this effort, you or your potential partner are expected to help prevent unsafe situations included, but not limited to threats made via face to face, telephone, text, fax, electronic or conventional mail or any other communication devices deemed unsafe will not be tolerated. The T.E.A.M philosophy plays a vital role in helping to attain and maintain a safe environment.

UNWELCOMED BEHAVIOR

You are committed to providing a serious and loving environment that is free from intimidation, discrimination, harassment, or hostility. Which includes anything verbal, physical, visual, or written that's unwanted. You should be against all individuals that initiate, participate, or witness tragic situations and do nothing to help or stop it. Unwanted behavior extends to all forms including race, color, religion, national origin, ancestry, age, physical, or mental disability, genetic characteristics, medical condition, sex, sexual orientation, marital status, racial slurs, ethnic slurs, demeaning comments or jokes.

INTERACTING WITH OTHERS

You are ladies and gentlemen working with ladies and gentlemen. If you want respect, you have to give respect. It all starts with you. You'll encounter people who have different views, opinions, and ideas. You'll also come in contact with people who are completely different from you, and you will need to be okay with that. To provide an environment where you can thrive, you should practice your T.E.A.M philosophy every day. It is a good practice when performed correctly, and it limits awkwardness and uncomfortable situations.

SAFE AND SOBER

It is your responsibility to help provide a safe, sober and productive environment for yourself, your potential partner, and others that you may come in contact with. The expectation for you is to perform all the basic functions of this relationship to the best of your ability. If you are impaired, often, this will alter your ability to perform effectively. You are not allowed to conduct any relationship business at any time while under the influence of alcohol or illegal drugs. If you are taking any prescribed medications or over-the-counter medication which may in any way impair your judgment, speech, actions, or performance; your potential partner needs to inform you right away.

PERSONAL CALLS, PAGERS, CELL PHONES

Cell phones and other electronic devices must be turned off while you are together unless agreed upon in advance. Personal calls may be made before and after your scheduled time together. The only exceptions are emergency calls. Keep in mind that your time together is your time to spend with one another.

BE ON TIME

It is important that you make every effort to be on time to all appointments, dates, scheduled time together or planned events. The method that you use to be on time should be of the highest honesty and integrity. Being on time is very important to the success of your relationship. If your potential partner is excessively late, this is a red flag and it may result in starting the Disciplinary Take Action System.

IF WE HAVE PLANS

It's essential to be aware of your time, attendance, and punctuality. If we schedule an outing, plan a trip, take vacations/holidays, or a special event together, it's essential that you are competent and efficient with managing your time. Tardiness or no show makes it difficult to manage your time effectively. Emergencies and or illnesses can and do arise, but, it is inexcusable to be late or absent without communication.

Just call if you are going to be late because time is money and you should believe that your time is valuable. If you are ill and will not be able to attend an outing, you are expected to call as soon as possible, preferably at least two to four hours before your scheduled time. Keep in mind that not calling and or not showing up may result in disciplinary action (explained later). Repeated incidents of being late or excessive absenteeism, whether excused or not, may result in disciplinary action, which could include separation of your relationship.

KEEPING YOUR POTENTIAL PARTNER INFORMED

When your potential partner joins your **T.E.A.M.**, they'll provide information that you believe is truthful. You are expected to keep each other informed and up-to-date on important information that may help or hurt the relationship. You need to keep each other promptly informed about changes in your telephone number, address, and employment. Also, and very important any changes on how you think, interact, or feel about the direction of the relationship.

CONFIDENTIALITY

During the relationship, your potential partner may have access to personal or confidential information regarding your relationships, friends, and family; such as names, numbers, and addresses, etc. The information you may receive is not to be shared with anyone without permission first, because sharing private information may result in disciplinary action up to and including separation.

GOING THROUGH YOUR THINGS

If your potential partner gives you any reason not to trust them, then you won't. You both reserve the right to inspect each other's things at any time without prior notice. This includes, but not limited to text messages, voice mail, e-mail, telephones, videos, wallets, backpacks, and purses. To avoid this, you should communicate often to avoid misunderstandings.

WORK ON YOUR MIND AND BODY

Sharpening your mind is very important to the success of your relationship. Earl Nightingale said, "A dull mind or imagination will lead to a dull and unimaginative life." Keep your mind sharp! Read, study, learn, practice, follow, join, or listen to something educational daily or as often as possible. Also; work on your body. I scanned the internet and found Coach Micah, and he said to use the 21/90 rule: it takes 21 days to create a habit, and it takes 90-days to create a new lifestyle.

EXTRACURRICULAR ACTIVITIES

_____

Your name

_____

Partner's Name

I completely disagree with you spending time with another person romantically while we're dating.

You should think seriously about the effects that such extracurricular activity may have on your future. Also, on your overall development and mental impact on your current relationship. You are being held to your word unless you give a reason to doubt. No exceptions!

RELATIONSHIPS ARE "AT WILL"

Remember your potential partner may depend on the quality of time and communication you provide. They may expect you to maintain a consistent level of feedback every day. If your potential partner cannot respect, support, or believe in your vision, then it is clear that the two of you are not going in the same direction with the relationship.

This red flag should swiftly, automatically, or speedily remind you that your potential partner is still on an "at-will" basis. Within the first 90-days of the probationary period, you reserve the right to bypass all or any steps of the disciplinary system and immediately separate yourself "at-will" with or without cause and notice.

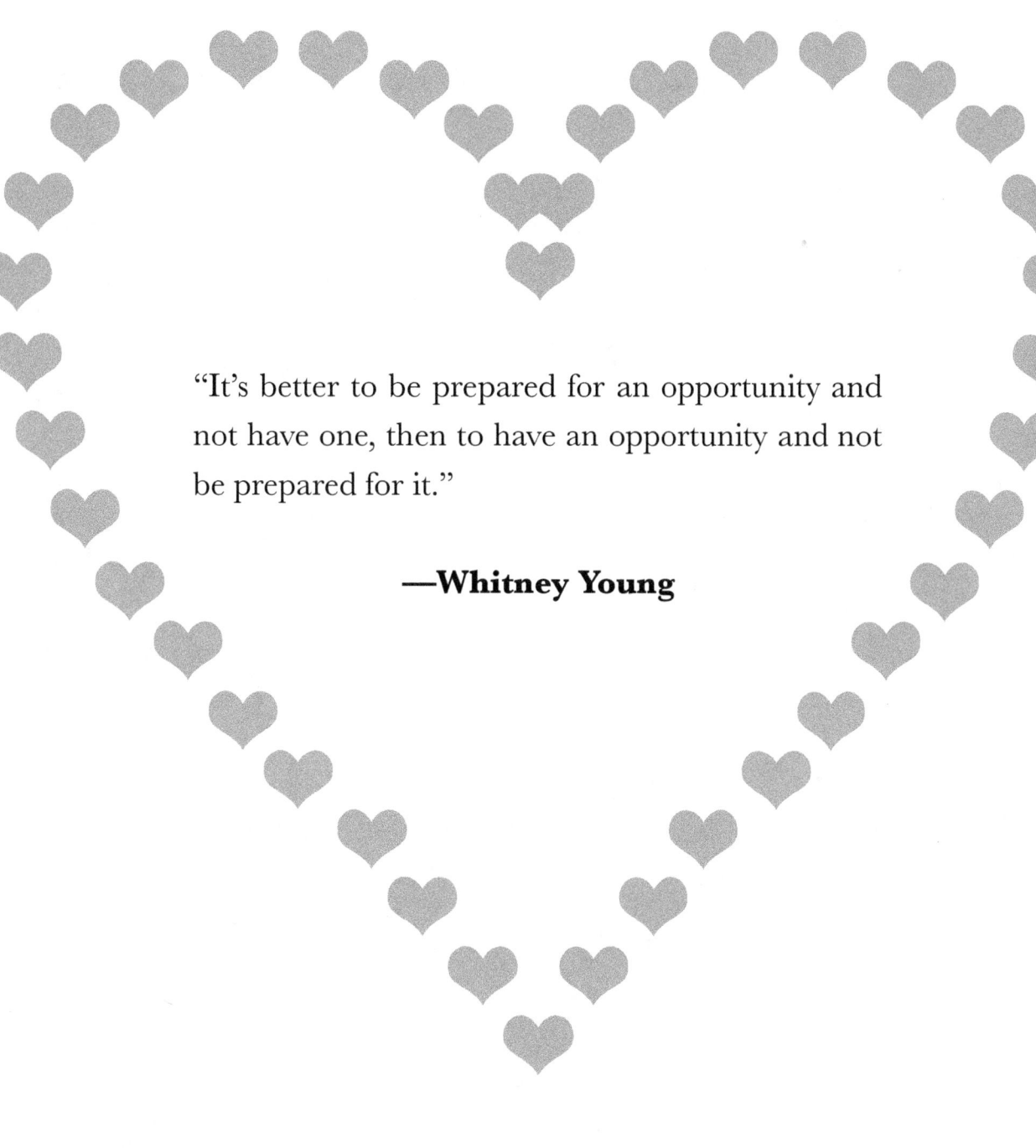

"It's better to be prepared for an opportunity and not have one, then to have an opportunity and not be prepared for it."

—Whitney Young

DON'T WANT VS. WANT?

If you ask the average person what type of romantic relationship they want, most will tell you what they don't want. According to a book by Shakti Gawain, titled, *Creative Visualization*, when you focus on what you don't want, it will continue to show up over and over again, even if you believe that you're pushing those negative thoughts away. Remember, you are not! That's why it's so very important to focus on the thoughts you want and stay away from negative thoughts of what you don't want.

Once you start to believe that your thoughts create your reality, things will change almost instantly. It is so much better to focus on what you want, not what you don't want. You should be clear, focused, and intentional on what you want to see in your love life. Keep in mind that once you become that person who is loving, love shows up every time, no exceptions.

You can use my examples below for some ideas to follow for the exercise at the end of this book. These examples will help you get clarity before starting your list to manifesting your ideal potential partner.

MY EXAMPLE: DON'T WANT

- I don't want someone that smokes
- I don't want someone that doesn't have reliable transportation.
- I don't want someone that's lazy

MY EXAMPLE: DO WANT

- I want someone that takes care of his/her body
- I want someone that has a car
- I want someone that's ambitious

NOTES

BE SPECIFIC ABOUT WHAT YOU WANT

Many of us know what it's like to choose the wrong person to be in a relationship. Unfortunately, it's a common experience to feel like you don't make the right decisions when it comes to relationships. You either think you don't know how to tell if someone's right for you to begin with, or after you've chosen a partner; only to find out that it wasn't a good match toward the end of the relationship. This feeling of possibly not knowing how to choose the right person can make dating scary!

If you don't trust yourself to choose well, you're bound to feel uneasy and unsure when looking for "The One." We all know that to be in this position is not good. So, is there a way to be sure that the person you're choosing is right for you? I believe there is.

In my experience, it is nice to know what you want, but with that said; stay open, because I have seen so many times with past clients, the person that they married, turned out to be a completely different person from "the one" they were dating.

MY EXAMPLE OF WANTS FOR MY POTENTIAL PARTNER:

Language(s): English, as a first or second language

Employment Type: Working Entrepreneur or Full Time Employment

Education Level Required: Some College or College Graduate

Relationship Experience (in years): minimum of 3 years

Average Yearly Salary: $50,000 or more

Bonus: Since of Humor, Hopeless Romantic, Can Cook

Religion: Not important but, Prefer Christian and must Love God

Preferred Age: 30–55

Preferred Sex: Female

Height: (Not important but, prefer between 5.2–5.9)

Weight: Not Important but, prefer a healthy weight

Body Style: Average to Athletic.

Race: Not important

Ambition: Needs to be at least somewhat ambitious

Does your potential partner like kids? Yes. **Why?** I would like to have one or two kids someday, I don't have any but I'm open to the discussion about it.

How often does your potential partner work out? Two to three times a week. **Why?** Good health is important to me and for the longevity of our future.

Do you expect your potential partner to be a leader? Yes. **Why?** I want someone to take control of situations big or small at times when needed. I also want someone to hold me accountable and not let me play small in life.

Do you want your potential partner to be a book reader? Absolutely Yes. **Why?** Reading is attractive, it is sexy to me especially if you choose to read to me.

NOTES

BEST RELATIONSHIP PRACTICES

Everybody has different beliefs they value in relationships, and those values govern how you treat yourself and others. Always keep in mind that "A RELATIONSHIP IS A JOB AND A JOB AIN'T NOTHING BUT WORK."™ It's important to state your values first to give a crystal-clear understanding of your expectations. You should always strive to be the change in the world that you want to see. Here are some values that you can practice every day.

- **Practice Smiling and Have Fun**
  It's a good thing that you take "YOUR RELATIONSHIP" very seriously, and yourself lightly. Experience will teach you that people enjoy knowing that you are serious about what you want in your relationship, and you can still find humor in your daily lives and the joy of living it. **Practice the Golden Rule:** Treat others the way they

want to be treated not the way you believe or feel they should be treated, because you may not know their history.

- **Practice How to Use Respect**
Be the change that you want to see in the world. As an example, you should always demonstrate consideration, acceptance, and appreciation of all people's diversity, ideas, beliefs, and feelings at all times.

- **Practice How to Trust Yourself**
You are encouraged to express yourself freely in communication, thoughts, and ideas. You are encouraged to speak and act honestly with me and everyone. You are encouraged to follow through on all your commitments.

- **Practice T.E.A.M Success**
Together–Everyone–Achieves–More. You should practice excellence in yourself, regardless of your circumstances or situation. Practice going above and beyond expectations with your potential partner. Practice effective communication with your friends, loved ones, and anyone that you come in contact.

NOTES

PERSONAL APPEARANCE

Your appearance is important to me, and my appearance should be important to you as well. How we represent ourselves is equally important, and our image should matter. You are responsible for maintaining your image or appearance without being told to do so. Therefore, I reserve the right to define what choices of appearance and grooming (i.e., hygiene, hairstyles, facial hair, and jewelry) are acceptable and appropriate based on my opinion and the image I want to represent.

MY EXAMPLES OF PERSONAL APPEARANCE:

General Guidelines
- **Hair** – Should be clean, neat and conservative with no extreme styling or hair color whether it's long or short hair unless agreed on prior.

- **Face** – Females must not wear heavy or unnatural looking make-up. Males must be clean shaven. A neatly trimmed mustache, goatee, beard, and sideburns must be neatly trimmed, and should not exceed the bottom of the ear lobe.

- **Personnel Hygiene** – Bath or shower daily, and fresh breath is required. The use of chewing gum is acceptable in a desperate situation. Wash your hand after using the restroom, every time.

- **Tattoos** – Are acceptable but not excessive.

- **Nails** – Should be clean, or manicured and/or pedicured.

- **Shoes & Clothes** – Shoes must be clean and in good condition. Clothes must be clean, stain free, and with no offensive writing, colors, or letters.

- **Jewelry** – is acceptable but not excessive.

TIP: ACCEPTABILITY IS SUBJECTIVE TO THE INDIVIDUAL'S DISCRETION.

"The road that leads everything back to the beginning, where and how it all started is with communication."

—Tamara Campbell

INTENTIONAL COMMUNICATION

Creating an open line of communication is an essential part of developing a successful relationship. In keeping the lines of communication open, you are encouraging your potential partner to come to you first with any issue or problem that may affect your relationship.

It is imperative to talk frequently about your relationship in the beginning. I encourage you to set time aside to check-in with your potential partner at least once a week. Especially in the first 90-days and beyond to discuss the direction of your relationship. Keep it simple. Ask questions, such as, "What worked this week?" and "What didn't work and how can we improve?"

MY EXAMPLES OF INTENTIONAL COMMUNICATION:
If your partner is doing something that irritates you, let's say they leave dirty dishes in the sink. You could say, "I love it when you come over and visit, and I enjoy spending time with you. I was wondering if you could clean your dish

or put it in the dishwasher after your done and not just leave it in the sink. Your consideration saves me so much time at night before I go to bed."

You've respectfully addressed the issue in a loving way, communicating that you still appreciate your potential partner, but at the same time you are getting your message across. If there's still a problem after the initial one or two talks in one week, and you believe your issue remains unresolved, change up your strategy before giving up or contact outside help. Here are some tactics you can use to facilitate better communication between you and your potential partner.

- **Listen or learn to listen from the heart**
  A good listener stays focused on the topic at hand and listens to what the other person is saying. Often in conversation, it's tempting to let your mind wander or think about what you're going to say next. Stay present and stay engaged in the conversation.

- **Open door policy**
  This policy means that your potential partner can approach you with any questions, issues, comments, or concerns at any time. It will help build trust between you and your potential partner. The open-door policy also shows that you are open to hearing what they have to say, and it ultimately shows that you are approachable and willing to listen.

- **Encourage Feedback**
  Your potential partner should ask for feedback regularly. It is especially important when implementing a new program, project, or task to help strengthen your relationship. Ask your potential partner if they fully understood your message. Keep in mind that their feedback may come

across as a positive or a negative message. If it's negative, try not to take it personally. Remember, you're still trying to learn each other. Use the feedback to help improve your relationship.

- **Concentrate on Your Body Language**

    You may not realize it that you communicate with your body language as much as with your mouth. Keep in mind that certain gestures and postures convey a specific message or attitude. Folding your arms shows that you are defensive. Looking away or not making eye contact shows you are disinterested or distracted in what the other person is saying. Being aware of body language will help you to maintain open lines of communication.

- **Straightforward & Direct communication**

    Try not to beat around the bush or sugar coat your communication even if it's good news. You can believe that after 90 days, your potential partner will respect your honesty, even if they do not agree with the message you are giving them.

Communication Goes Two Ways

Always reach out to your potential partner and don't wait for them to come to you. Continue to ask questions that will benefit your relationship and the direction you want it to go. The intention is to ensure that things are running smoothly. If there is a problem or issue, address it right away. When resolving problems or issues, try to avoid swearing, using slang, or implied communications.

You should teach or encourage your potential partner to always come to you first with any issues about the relationship. Some men and women are not initially comfortable communicating when trust has not been established. Perhaps your potential partner never experienced encouragement to open up about their emotions. However, by letting them know they are free to speak their minds and it's confidential. I believe it will help to keep the lines of communication open.

NOTES

JEALOUSY

You have to be committed to providing an environment that is free from jealousy, intimidation, hostility, discrimination, and harassment of any kind. Jealously can show up verbally, physically, visually, or written. Any form of jealously will not be tolerated and will be addressed immediately. You should be firmly against all type of harassment.

If you feel, believe, or witness someone including yourself subjected to jealously by anyone that's personally connected to you or your potential partner, you are encouraged to quickly address this issue or report all the facts right away to someone you trust and/or can help. All parties involved will get together as soon as possible to discuss what's the best cause of action?

NOTES

KEEP AGGRESSIVE BEHAVIOR AWAY

Keep in mind that aggressive behavior could be displayed by anyone, anywhere, and at any time and sometimes without warning. You should always do your best to ensure the safety of anyone directly connected to you. Your potential partner may not possess any weapons without your knowledge while you are together. This includes but not limited to, firearms, knives, or anything concealed that's labeled as a weapon. There are some personal defense items such as mace and pepper spray that is considered acceptable. Aggression may associate with other symptoms that are determined by an underlying disorder or illness. Ailments that influence behavior may have psychological, cognitive, and physical symptoms. Some additional signs and symptoms may include:

- Anxiety
- Moodiness
- Agitation

- Stress
- Financial problems
- Personal or family illness, disputes and or disagreements
- Depression
- Poor communication skills due to negativity
- Trouble with language comprehension, writing or reading
- Impaired judgment and decision making
- Insomnia
- Threatening behavior

Never become involved in a potentially aggressive situation that could potentially jeopardize your safety and the safety of others. In the event that you are confronted with a potential aggressive situation I suggest a peaceful solution or if you are able to dial 911, do so immediately.

NOTES

UNACCEPTABLE BEHAVIOR, CONDUCT, OR ATTITUDE

In order for you to succeed in this very competitive world locally or internationally you must maintain a high standard of conduct at all times. If your potential partner chooses to engage in any conduct that is contrary to the best interests of your relationship, then they may be subjected to disciplinary action ranging from verbal or written communication but not limited to separation. The agreement that the two of you have is a mutual agreement and either one can sever the relationship at any time with or without cause or advance notice.

MY EXAMPLE OF UNACCEPTABLE BEHAVIOR, CONDUCT, OR ATTITUDE:

- Verbal abuse, actual physical violence, foul language, and rude behavior toward another person regardless of who started it.

- Destroying or damaging someone's property or materials.
- Refusing to follow the rules, directions, policy, or procedures that were agreed upon.
- Unauthorized possession of items, removal of items that don't belong to you, or using things regardless of its size or shape without permission.
- Our agreement regarding any form of harassment, illegal drugs, excessive use of alcohol, bad attitude, concealed weapons, and excessive tardiness.

NOTES

PROGRESSIVE COMMUNICATION TAKE ACTION SYSTEM

The Progressive Communication Take Action System is where the penalties increase upon repeat occurrences, rather than an immediate separation for a first misunderstanding like disagreements or minor arguments. This system will ensure that your potential partner is treated in a manner that's consistent and fair. This disciplinary system is designed to change old habits and bad behavior to create new and improved ones.

You are expected to always enforce policies and procedures to help improve your relationship and stop misconduct from occurring through a variety of disciplinary procedures appropriate to the circumstances. Action steps are always in chronological order. So, if your potential partner condones, tolerates, or participates in behavior that's mentioned in the above content, this may result in the swift and the immediate start of the Progressive Communication Take Action System. NO EXCEPTIONS!

<u>The Progressive Communication Take Action System consists of 3 actions steps:</u>
1. **Verbal Communication**
2. **Written Communication**
3. **Separation**

1. Verbal Communication

This is the first conversation that you have with your potential partner about performance, behavior, bad habits, and/or conduct. This verbal communication gives notice to your potential partner that this issue is serious and must be corrected right away. Your verbal language and non-verbal language should be the same when communicating with your potential partner. Before concluding the conversation make sure that your potential partner understands that if this issue or related issues are not resolved in a timely manner, it can lead to further disciplinary actions up to and including separation.

2. Written Communication

If this is the second communication or warning that you have with your potential partner about the same issue(s) or related issue(s) that have been unresolved then progression is inevitable. By this time you should have had at least one or two personal conversations or coaching sessions to help improve your potential partner's chances for a successful start in your relationship.

If your potential partner isn't willing to turn things around then a written communication form should be given to your potential partner right away. Remember to only write what happened and only state the facts, never use your opinion(s). Only include what is currently discussed, and a realistic timeline to correct the infraction(s). This particular communication form is very serious because your potential partner knows that this could be the final notice that he or she may receive before separation happens.

3. Separation

I have only seen two outcomes using progressive communication take-action action system where the potential partner was finally able to turn things around and all issues were resolved. I hope your potential partner can turn things around. However, if all else fails, the only remaining course of action is separation. The final written communication form is open-ended so no further written warnings need to be given. If given another chance and your potential partner corrects the issue for a month or two and then the issue returns there is no need to start the progressive communication take action system all over again. At this point, you need to seriously decide if the relationship is worth preserving. Keep in mind that separating from your potential partner is one of the hardest things you will ever do. But it comes with "The Job" and you have to do it.

NOTES

"A good relationship is when someone accepts your past, supports your present, and encourages your future."

—Zig Ziglar

The Relationship Job
EXERCISE BOOK

The exercises will help you get crystal-clear about your standards and what your non-negotiables are. The exercises in this workbook are for individuals who are seriously ready to do "the work" in order to have a higher, next level relationship.

Remember:
A RELATIONSHIP IS A JOB
AND A JOB AIN'T NOTHING BUT WORK!™

DON'T WANT VS. WANT?

One of the hardest questions to ask yourself is, what do I really want in the person that I may spend the rest of my life with. Most of time you don't even know that you are with the "wrong person" until the "right person" shows up, and you can't even remember how you got through your life without them. Are there actual ways to be sure that the person you are going to choose is a right fit for you? I believe their is.

    Write down below what you want and please be as specific as you can, this will help you get started on manifesting your potential partner.

Write all the things that you DON'T want to see in your potential partner:

_____

_____

_____

_____

Write all the things that you DO want to see in your potential partner:

___

___

___

___

BE SPECIFIC ABOUT WHAT YOU WANT

It's time to stop making excuses for not getting what you want. It's time to be very deliberate about what you really want. Below is an exercise for you to see what you are attracting into your experience. Being intentional is extremely important. If you make mediocre choices in what you want, you can expect mediocre results. However, if you choose to be honest in deciding what's most important to you and the success of your relationship, you can expect to accomplish your objectives. I want to encourage you not to ignore your inner thoughts. I know firsthand how exhausting it is to continuously ignore that "little voice." Ladies and gentlemen, the "little voice" is real. It's alerting you to stop wasting valuable time and energy and get what you deserve. It's time to be crystal-clear about what you really want. Please write what you want and be very specific.

If you don't trust yourself to choose well, you're bound to feel uneasy and unsure when looking for "The One." We all know that's not a good position to be in. So, is there actually a way to be sure that the person you're choosing is right for you? I believe there is.

You can follow this list below for some ideas; of how to get your list started before manifesting your potential partner. In my experience it is nice to know exactly what you want, but with that said; stay open, because I have seen so many times with past clients, the person that they married, turned out to be a completely different person from "the one" they were dating.

MY EXAMPLES OF WANTS AND DON'T WANTS:
Language(s): _____
Employment Type: Doctor / Lawyer / Executive / Entrepreneur / Chef / Other: _____
Education Level Required: Diploma / GED / Degree / Some College / Other: _____
Relationship Experience (in years): 1–5 / 6–10 / 10 or more
Average Yearly Salary: 25,000 / 50,000 / 75,000 / 100,000 or above
Religion: _____
Preferred Age: _____   **Preferred Sex:** _____
Height: _____   **Weight:** _____
Body Style: Athletic / Muscular / Average / BBW / BBM
Race: Black / White / Asian / Latin / Other: _____
Hair color: _____   **Eye color:** _____
Tattoos: Yes / No / Maybe   **Ambition:** Yes / No / Maybe
Does your potential partner like or want kids? Yes / No
Why is this important to you or not?

_____

_____

_____

THE RELATIONSHIP JOB

Does your potential partner exercise or work out regularly?
Yes / No
Why is this important to you or not?

_____

_____

_____

How honest do you expect your potential partner to be with you? On a scale of 1–10 (#1. meaning you are ok with a little mystery and #10 means I want to be informed about everything, everyday!)
Why is this important to you or not?

_____

_____

_____

Do you want your potential partner to be a leader? Yes / No
Why is this important to you or not?

_____

_____

_____

Do you want your potential partner to be a book reader?
Yes / No
Why is this important to you or not?

_____

_____

_____

BEST RELATIONSHIP PRACTICES

It's important that you state your values and how often you practice those values. Everybody has different values they practice in their relationships and these practices should teach us how to treat you, how we should treat ourselves, and others. Always be crystal clear with yourself when you explain your values, your expectations, your daily routines, and practices to your potential partner. Below write your core relationship values that you can practice every day.

<u>Write everything that's fun, enjoyable, and important to you, that you want your partner to value as well.</u>

Remember to practice:

PERSONAL APPEARANCE

Your potential partner's appearance is important, and how they represent themselves is equally important. Your potential partner is responsible for maintaining their personal image and appearance without being told to do so. If he/she is unclear about your standards, remember you reserve the right to define what choices of appearance and grooming (i.e., hygiene, hairstyles, facial hair and jewelry) are acceptable.

Write down everything that you expect from your potential partner:

• **Hair**

_____

_____

- **Face**

_____

_____

- **Personnel Hygiene**

_____

_____

- **Tattoos**

_____

_____

- **Nails**

_____

_____

- **Shoes & Clothes**

_____

_____

- **Jewelry**

_____

_____

JEALOUSLY

You should be committed to providing an environment that is free from jealousy. This includes intimidation, hostility, discrimination, or harassment. Jealously may be verbal, physical, visual or written. Any form of jealously will be addressed immediately. You should be strongly against any form of jealously.

Write down what's not acceptable and what you will not tolerate:

_____

_____

_____

_____

_____

KEEP AGGRESSIVE BEHAVIOR AWAY

Keep in mind that most aggressive behavior starts off very subtle. The signs are usually always there, and if they're not addressed immediately it may get out of control. Aggressive behavior can happen to anyone, anywhere, at any time, and the majority of the time it happens without warning. You are responsible for your own safety and anyone directly connected to you.

Write down different signs that may trigger aggressive behavior in you and in your potential partner as well.

_____

_____

_____

BE THE CHANGE THAT YOU WANT TO SEE

If you have read "The Relationship Job™" it's likely because you're tired of an ordinary relationship and you want an extraordinary one. If someone gave you this handbook as a gift, they probably believe you deserve a happy, healthy, committed, and long-term relationship. My hope for you is that you create what you want to see in your next, new, or current relationship. "The Relationship Job™" is your handbook to use it as a guide. I urge you not to let it sit and collect dust! "The Relationship Job™" should be used as a living document and guide, to be revisited and updated at least annually. Even if you are in a happy and successful relationship, "The Relationship Job™" will be helpful. It's tailored to fit and reflect the relationship you really want.

I acknowledge, understand, and agree with the information above. I will comply, communicate, participate, and/or delegate the above information to my potential partner.

_____
Your Name (Please Print)

_____
Potential Partner's Name (Please Print)

_____
Your Signature

_____
Potential Partner's Signature

_____
Date

EVALUATIONS

2 WEEKS – 30 DAYS – 60 DAYS – 90 DAYS

The evaluations are designed to be a shared experience. You will need two copies, one for you and one for your potential partner. You should evaluate each other at the same time. The scoring is for you to see where the two of you are in the relationship.

Scoring range from 1–5.
1 = Never (never try to improve)
2 = Sometimes (sometimes improve, but without a since of urgency)
3 = Most of the time (improves most of the time but still need coaching or developing)
4 = Mostly Every time (want to improve, mostly every time with minimum supervision)
5 = Every time (is always improving, never settling, above average)

You can only ask two questions as you go line by line while doing the evaluation.
#1. "Why" did you score me at this number?
#2. "How" do I increase my lower score to a higher score?

<u>Listen to the answers – don't speak – don't disagree – don't argue – and most importantly don't add your opinions, even if you don't like what you are hearing, just keep listening.</u>

Keep in mind; if you agree with the low score that your partner gave you then, simply ask your partner (example: if your partner scored you at a 2, all you can ask is <u>how do I get from a 2 to a 3?</u> Then work on that for a week. After a week get back together and evaluate each other's progress, if all is good then the only question you should ask now is <u>how do I get from a 3 to a 4?</u> Then go work on that for a week. Do this every week until you reach a number that the two of you are comfortable with. <u>This should take about 4 weeks to complete each evaluations excluding the 2 week evaluation. If you are unsure about him/her before the two weeks evaluation, separation should be immediate.</u>

If you get what you believe is a low score (this is where the fun really kicks in). The idea is to keep building up and improving for one another until the two of you are at number that you both can agree upon. After you've agreed on a number there are no more negotiations. You can no longer settle for less. Neither of you can lower your expectations at any cost. PERIOD! **FYI:** If you believe that you need to evaluate your potential partner separately for any reason and you do not want to make it a shared experience please do. **<u>You must evaluate fairly.</u>** Because; there are no perfect people so if you are looking for something to be wrong you may prematurely convince yourself that you found something that's not really there.

Something to think about; if your potential partner has not improved in an agreed upon time then its best to think that he/she may not have potential. If you are on the fence about your potential partner, then ask yourself.

THE RELATIONSHIP JOB

1. **Does your potential partner understand how to improve?** (If the answer is no then you may owe it to him/her to possibly help them to get better or improve).
2. **Does your potential partner care to improve?** (If your answer is no, then you are unable to help him/her improve at this moment in time).
3. **Does it seem that your potential partner will never improve?** (If the answer is yes do not waste any more of your time! At this point separation should be unavoidable or inevitable.

2-WEEK EVALUATION

SCORE:

1 = Never

2 = Sometimes

3 = Most of the time

4 = Mostly Every time

5 = Every time

THE ONLY CONSIDERATION IS, YOUR POTENTIAL PARTNER
NEEDS TO SCORE AT LEAST 80% OR BETTER

		Score
	Self	Potential Partner
1) Lead by Example (1–5 points each. 25 points total):		
Is your potential partner able to accept constructive criticism?		
Is your potential partner motivated and/or a self-starter?		
Do you believe that your potential partner contribution(s) will add to the value of the relationship?		
Does your potential partner say what they mean and mean what they say?		
Is your potential partner aware and respectful of your time?		
2) Accountability (1–5 points each. 25 points total):	Self	Potential Partner
Does your potential partner communicate with you effectively?		
Does your potential partner allow pride or ego to get in the way when you ask about issues or concerns?		
Does your potential partner ask for help when needed, and doesn't act like they have to do everything alone?		
Is your potential partner financially responsible?		
Do you believe your potential partner will push you or help you complete your goals or projects?		

3) Personal Development (1–5 points each. 25 points total):	Self	Potential Partner
Does your potential partner have a plan for the direction of his/her life?		
Is your potential partner comfortable with public display of affection?		
Does your potential partner ensure that his/her health is kept in good condition through eating and/or personal fitness?		
Does your potential partner bath or clean his/her body and wear clean cloths regularly?		
Do you feel your potential partner will make good decisions for the relationship when you're not present?		
4) Attitude (1–25 Points. 25 points total):	**Self**	**Potential Partner**
Does your potential partner display the type of attitude that you consider positive? (1–25pts)		
TOTAL		

30-DAY EVALUATION

SCORE:

1 = Never

2 = Sometimes

3 = Most of the time

4 = Mostly Every time

5 = Every time

THE ONLY CONSIDERATION IS, YOUR POTENTIAL PARTNER NEEDS TO SCORE AT LEAST 80% OR BETTER

	Score	
	Self	Potential Partner
1) Lead by Example (1–5 points each. 25 points total):		
Does your potential partner understand all of your standards and guidelines?		
Is your potential partner someone you can open up to and speak freely with?		
Does your potential partner live within his/her financial means?		
Does your potential partner achieve most objectives and goals that he/she sets?		
Is your potential partner helpful and/or fill in where they are needed and does so without an attitude?		
2) Accountability (1–5 points each. 25 points total):	Self	Potential Partner
Is your potential partner respectful to you with his/her communication?		
Does your potential partner ensure that pride, ego, and arrogance are suppressed?		
Is your potential partner romantic or does chivalrous things?		
Does your potential partner hold themselves accountable for all their successes as well as their failures?		
Does your potential partner use your ideas or opinions when making decisions for the relationship?		

3) Personal Development (1–5 points each. 25 points total):	Self	Potential Partner
Does your potential partner believe in a 50/50 relationship or 100/100 relationship?		
Does your potential partner read books or develop his / her mind as often as possible?		
Does your potential partner continue to ensure that his/her health is kept in good condition through eating and personal fitness?		
Does your potential partner respect you and themself equally?		
Does your potential partner manage their time wisely?		
4) Attitude (1–25 Points. 25 points total):	**Self**	**Potential Partner**
Does your potential partner communicate with you and others in a respectful way, without screaming, yelling, or the use of sarcasm, or profanity.		
TOTAL		

60-DAY EVALUATION

SCORE:

1 = Never

2 = Sometimes

3 = Most of the time

4 = Mostly Every time

5 = Every time

THE ONLY CONSIDERATION IS, YOUR POTENTIAL PARTNER NEEDS TO SCORE AT LEAST 80% OR BETTER

	Score Self	Score Potential Partner
1) Lead by Example (1–5 points each. 25 points total):		
Does your potential partner understand and respect what you value?		
Does your potential partner get along with your friends & family and their friends & family?		
Does your potential partner ensure that you and everyone you associate with feels welcomed?		
Is your potential partner comfortable with uncomfortable conversations?		
Does your potential partner make responsible decisions?		
2) Accountability (1–5 points each. 25 points total):	Self	Potential Partner
Does your potential partner take ownership for his/her happiness?		
Does your potential partner have an outgoing personality?		
Does your potential partner take care of all of his/her business including bills, receipts, and appointments in a timely manner?		
Does your potential partner meet your emotional needs?		
Does your potential partner like or enjoy spending time with you?		

	Self	Potential Partner
3) Personal Development (1–5 points each. 25 points total):		
Where does your potential partner see themself in the next five years?		
Is your potential partner attentive and present while listening?		
Is your potential partner an example of a good role model?		
Does your potential partner respect you and themself equally?		
Does your potential partner continue to pay attention to his/her personal hygiene at all times?		
4) Attitude (1–25 Points. 25 points total):	Self	Potential Partner
Does your potential partner understand how "T.E.A.M. work" works? "Together," Everyone, Achieves, More? (1–25pts)		
TOTAL		

90-DAY EVALUATION

SCORE:

1 = Never

2 = Sometimes

3 = Most of the time

4 = Mostly Every time

5 = Every time

THE ONLY CONSIDERATION IS, YOUR POTENTIAL PARTNER NEEDS TO SCORE AT LEAST 80% OR BETTER

	Score	
	Self	Potential Partner
1) Lead by Example (1–5 points each. 25 points total):		
Does your potential partner get upset or irritated with you easily?		
Does your potential partner wait until he/she is told what to do before taking action?		
Does your potential partner stimulate your mind?		
Does your potential partner show confidence in their verbal, mental, and physical abilities?		
Does your potential partner still promote what you believe is a positive attitude?		
2) Accountability (1–5 points each. 25 points total):	Self	Potential Partner
Does your potential partner continue to communicate with you effectively?		
Does your potential partner allow pride or ego get in the way with issues about your concerns?		
Does your potential partner meet your mental and/or intellectual needs?		
Is your potential partner smart with matters involving money?		
Is your potential partner aware of his/her punctuality?		

3) Personal Development (1–5 points each. 25 points total):	Self	Potential Partner
Does your potential partner have a plan for the direction of his/her life?		
Is your potential partner still comfortable with public display of affection?		
Does your potential partner continue to ensure that his/her health is kept in good condition through eating and personal fitness?		
If your potential partner starts a project or goal, do they complete that project or goal?		
Do you continue to feel that your potential partner will do what is best for your relationship when you are not around?		
4) Attitude (1–25 Points. 25 points total):	Self	Potential Partner
Do you feel your potential partner earned your bonus package (You are the BONUS PACKAGE) or do you feel they need more time? (1–25pts)		
TOTAL		

PROGRESSIVE COMMUNICATION TAKE ACTION FORM

Partner or Potential Partner:

Name: _____ Communication Date: _____

Type of Violation(s)

- ○ Attendance/Punctuality Issue
- ○ Weapons
- ○ Cleanliness/Personal Appearance
- ○ Misconduct
- ○ Creating a Disturbance
- ○ Not being Truthful
- ○ Extracurricular Activities
- ○ Performance

- ○ Personal Development
- ○ Safety issues
- ○ Not keeping your word
- ○ Jealously
- ○ Drugs/Alcohol
- ○ Unwanted Behavior
- ○ Damaging Property
- ○ Other

Describe the situation or behavior:

_____

_____

_____

_____

NOTE: If further misconduct, issues, or problems continue, it may result in further disciplinary action, which may include immediate separation.

I acknowledge that I have read this fully and understand all the information provided.

Partner/
Potential Partners Signature: _____ Date: _____

Your Signature: _____ Date: _____

Remember: Give Praise, Thanks, and Congratulate in Public–Give Discipline, Correction, and/or Reprimand in Private.

ACKNOWLEDGMENTS

To my immediate family, the ones who always believe in me, and I love you so much for that:
- My mother Sarah Campbell
- My older brother Eric Campbell
- My "younger sister" Tammy Campbell, I use the words "younger sister" in quotations because, my "younger sister" and I are only 11 months apart in age. Her birthday is in April so, every year for one month she and I are the same age until my birthday in May.
- My niece Destiny Campbell-Booker
- My daughter Jynasis Campbell

To all my cousins, aunts, and uncles, there are way too many to name individually so I'll speak from my family tree:
- The Watts
- The Young's
- The Campbell's
- The Thomas's

- The Chinns'
- The Rhodes'
- The Mosses'

To my sister and brothers from another mother, the ones that I can turn to for help, for advice or, whenever times get rough:
- Maurice Coleman
- Jamerson Holloway
- Dani and Odis

To my extended family at:
- Momentum Education (LT 10 – 4-4-4-4)
- Toastmasters (Self-Mastery)
- Rocky Peaks (Celebrate Recovery)
- Living Praise Christian Center & M.O.V.E. MEN!!!
- The Covenant House (California)

REFERENCES

- From Wikipedia, the Free Encyclopedia
- marriage.com Shellie Warren April 26th, 2018
- by Kevin Johnston; CHRON Updated June 30, 2017
- Lakeland Behavioral Health System has been a leading treatment center for 30+ years serving children, adolescents & older adults struggling with a mental health disorder
- By Alison Doyle Updated March 18, 2018
- https://www.voices.com/blog/work/
- https://www.linkedin.com/pulse/what-does-your-job-mean-you-msc-mba-pmp-itil-cobit-cisa-edge
- https://what-happened-on.com/event/Mint+Julep+Day
- https://what-happened-on.com/event/Infidelity+SPeaKS+Awareness+Day
- https://www.daysoftheyear.com/days/2018/05/30/

NOTES

NOTES

NOTES

www.ingramcontent.com/pod-product-compliance
Lightning Source LLC
Chambersburg PA
CBHW081748100526
44592CB00015B/2337